Sheila Black

Iron, Ardent

Poems

∞

EDUCE PRESS

Educe Press
Butte, MT

Published in the United States of America
First Edition, 2016

Library of Congress Catalogue-in-Publication Data
Shelia Black 2016--
Iron, Ardent

ISBN: 978-0-9965716-4-7

Cover Illustration by Christine Martin

educepress.com
facebook.com/educepress
twitter.com/educepress

PRAISE FOR IRON, ARDENT

In *Iron, Ardent*, Sheila Black invites us into the working mind of a many-selved speaker—detailing the misfit, hushed rioter, resistor, lonelyheart, iron-willed, iron-boned woman who names the softest beauty and shame of an unquiet world. Black lures her reader to follow a dangerous thread onto "the unholy banks of blossom" and makes us feel right at home.

—Laurie Ann Guerrero, Poet Laureate of Texas

In a time when visceral content is rendered meaningless by television screens, Sheila Black's harsh and necessary poems jolt the reader into awareness, then a shocked understanding of the kind of human suffering that begins with physical pain and leads to conflicted emotions. In the world she describes "Everyone spoke in code, everyone lied," and the narrator of "Birthday" declares "I am the cricket sawing its legs to sing." With exquisite, lyrical language the reader is taken from a Brazilian cemetery to gritty Manhattan streets, and on to rural landscapes that are never at ease: all with their beauty, their lies. Like Christina Rossetti, Sheila Black sees the world for the Goblin Market it is.

—Sharon Olinka, Author of *Old Ballerina Club*

Reading Sheila Black's poems will take you back to the first time you heard the song, "Pretty in Pink," by the Psychedelic Furs, the five chords of the intro luring you into joy and longing, a sweetness and grief that made you want nothing more than to throw your school books into the air and run out into the sun, get in a car—any car—and drive to a place where no one could find you, your heart beating so fast it could almost gallop out of your mouth. And so, these poems, too, will bring you the memory of heartbreak and a poet's joy of language that explicitly, and implicitly, keeps asking, "What becomes of the lives we discard?" a question that means, ultimately, "What has my life become?" and you will hear, once again, that exquisite D-chord strumming all you were and all you ever wanted to be into one magnificent beat that no one but you can hear.

—Octavio Quintanilla, author of *If I go Missing*

for Candice Morrow and Connie Voisine

To Sarah! Our voice in AWP. Thank you for all the wonderful work you are doing — and not just with AWP.

Best —

Contents

That iron man was born like me,
And he was once an ardent boy;
He must have felt in infancy
The glory of a summer sky.

—Emily Bronte*, 16 Lines*, *The Ashley Ms.,* October 1837

I

Iron, Ardent

1.

Nights my father strapped me in
the body brace, the boots laced up to my
ankles. Between the bar of iron
holding my feet in perfect fifth position.

Around my waist, curved ribs
so I pictured myself held
all night by a man of iron—
purely indifferent to my nerves,
flaming through tropical heat.

Moths and mosquitoes pelted the nets
around me. The moon tiger burned
on the wicker chair. Birds chattered.
The bird-of-paradise shed its petals.
A flamboyant tree spread its twigs
—red, swollen, scab to flower.

And by the river I saw
the crippled hospital, the walls a distemper,
and the pitiful ones, in error, who must learn to
renounce the pleasures of ordinary life.
For what? I knew.

The birds kept chattering and I, confined,
split off from myself and rose up
to join them in the trees while
below the iron man rocked himself to sleep.

2.

Outside in the street there was the beggar with elephantiasis;
the leper, the neighbor with eyes milky blind.

And in the book the child with the hand reaching out
for the water.

Everyone spoke in code, everyone lied.

There were the invisible hospitals, the poor
who could be scattered like lice.

The lanterns made of tin cans, which transformed
a light to lace.

There was sharp knife for the mangoes, the machete
for the coconut.

There was Flora with the scar bisecting her face,
and the wide stitches along it, ones a child would make.

And the bottle of white liquor that burned.
And the doctor who smelled of tobacco, the boots

with iron bars along the bottom.
The leather boots that smelled of sweat.

And there was doll that was like a pretty girl.
Golden hair, stiff limbs, and bird-button eyes.

And the world of the night, and the smell of jasmine
and a frozen dust. A bicycle riding along a moonlit track.

The ocean. The beach where Einstein proved his
Theory of Relativity, which meant there were many rooms, angles,

which meant that the clock, too, lied.
Back under the mosquito net. Back inside the moon,

and the house ticking, ticking.

And the wire corset, and the steel brace whose function was
to correct and straighten.

3.

(Paicambu Cemetary)

So many of us: Blind girl with tin
can, man with elephantiasis,
his leg a familiar monster. Across
the street from our house, the
high gates of the municipal cemetery.

Every weekend, the family
parties—thick sheaves of gladioli,
sinister sweetness. I perched on a
hollow in a wall, the bleaching
in yellow stone where a saint's likeness
had been. A reaching out, *a beseeching,*
arms that were not there.

A woman fell, rending the black net
of her hat. She was beautiful and
this mattered. Sunlight passing over me
as over the jacaranda. The graphite-colored
ants carried on their slow migrations,
eating whatever was in their path. Orchids
dangled white and crimson. Inside,
a city of child-sized houses.

I put my ear to the wall, tried to hear
the dead. Heard nothing, and then
a slow creaking, unleashing, the
way stories begin.

4.

She made me drunk—
that moon so open,
slid up inside
the dark sluice
of the sky. As if
she kept turning
toward me, kept
whispering "here,
no *here*, " until
I grew
concerned that
only I changed.
Where were her
wrinkles, where were
her eyes dimmed
with the sight
of too many roads,
so many houses
with fences, curtains,
those people with Milky
Ways inside them?
Moon just kept
her mouth open
as always, calling
the tides—and who
knew how?
A pull inside
me as I lifted the lens,
thread that will always
be part broken.
I pictured
her as a city
which contained
the relics, a dust, brittle,
and unused & they
remained inside. The
woman astronomer
who fed her brother like

a bird and she
the first to glimpse the
celestial firmament,
not as God's ceiling,
but an ocean of wrecks
and Sargasso, alive,
changeling, which she
would learn to read
alone, in pained solitude,
Moon singing
always to herself.

5.

The color of nylons without legs—
the smoke pulled in, mine.

My parents walked the beach at Imbituba,
drawing circles of fire under the sky

Einstein used to prove that time and
space are parts of the same house.

On the road down the mountain,
the restaurant where the owner

slit his throat with a machete,
and the throats of his wife and children.

Often I played with his daughter
in the waterfall that cut a crooked path

down the rock face behind their house.
Plate-sized flowers grew there, each with

a cool spot of water in its red-and-white cup.
We stripped a Barbie doll naked

and held its pale plastic legs
under the curtain of water as though

it could feel. I was not supposed to know
she was dead, but even when the

restaurant reopened for the tourists from
São Paulo, the new owner setting out

tables canopied in cloths like the flag—green,
yellow, *Ordem, Progreso*; we never stopped.

And when my parents vanished up the
beach (a noise of waves cast through

the dimming air), and I stopped to take a
first taste from my father's discarded

butt: Not smoke only but a space inside
that hungered to be filled. I knew

I would choose that slow falling,
carving of breath to feed a death

inside me. Her father, who once
said to my mother that where they lived

was the Garden of Eden.

6.

A journey to dread:
Persephone in the light of growing things—

crocus, daffodil, lily-of-the-valley
and its scent like the breath of mortal

babes. Early March, the dullard stars
drift down to be caught in

crab-apple, those unholy banks of blossom,
the river lined with willows, trailing

hands into mirror-water. On the second
floor, my recurring dream in the

house where they haul in the beached
ships. *My hair around*

me like blood from my body. Mud
and heat—the solidity of flesh,

my body that will ache, bend,
and, once broken, flower strangely.

7.

Madame Hansberry explained in her *Français*
parfait the mysteries of conjugation, the twists of

tense—for instance *le passé imparfait*, which

meant memory was a country. And one might enter it
knowingly, repeatedly—a dour closet feel in all those *woulds*
and *oftens* or every day the way we *would* stroll the

playground to the border of the tennis courts, clutch fists
to the chicken wire fence, wishing for someone to love, though

love like memory is difficult to access or
retain.

*

Madame Hansberry told us stories—remarkable stories of
people she had known, places she had lived.

Her brilliant niece died too
young, a rare cancer, but not before she sang a
raisin in the sun.

Who is not on the run? Madame Hansberry asked us,
who does not know what it is to be

defenestrated, kicked out, rootless; who does

not stroll the playgrounds of junior high, hands in
linty pockets, drafting secret messages in the margins?

*

Madame Hansberry spoke of Jim Crow days

"I had been to Paris but they could not have cared
less," she said, her sharp black eyes

battering against our dull faces like a bird trapped
in a room of mirrors—or unable to tell mirror

from sky. While she spoke, Gregory tossed paper airplanes,
beautiful worrisome Marie outlined her lips with, black
eye pencil, stabbed it into her open palm. Louis, behind me,

threatened to set fire to his hair. I put my hands
over my eyes. "Myth," said Madame Hansberry, "can often be

consolation." She said her favorite words in French
were the ones that could not be
translated. We asked her for an example. She said:

"This one: '*se dechire*,' which means 'to shred oneself,'"
and she laughed.

*

Madame Hansberry did not admire my command of French,
my punctuation, way with accents. On the first and last full-length

essay I wrote for her, on Racine's great (and to me deadly dull)
play *Phèdre*, she wrote "You have a decent grasp of

the large emotions, but you certainly lack proper discipline."

She said another favorite word of hers was 'chicanery.'

"Pretty as wrought iron isn't it," she beamed, "It means

shiny-bright, flim-flam, it means trickery." She lifted up
her thin finger, crooked it at us. "It means you WILL be
betrayed. It means you will lose who or

what or whatsoever you love."

*

She talked on, but we did not appear to listen—we knew she

was not talking to us any longer, some odd sense of
discretion that made us look away. I would have said I didn't

hear a single word she spoke, but that proved not to be
the case, for, later, behind the volleyball court where the sewer

ran and the elm trees yellowed, dying slowly of
that odd, not-really-Dutch disease, I repeated under

my breath "Myth, often, consolation," decided mine

would be the myth of Daphne—the junior high version, where
no one looked at me, no one pursued, no one

noticed me gone until I was already tree,

my branches
shivering in the rain or snapping lose in any storm.

8.

It must have been criminal, but saying
that tells nothing. There were candles;
there was the ruined house, which

like a house in a fairy tale gave the promise
of everything, the water-soaked plaster

the warped floors. Say he was thirty-nine and a
junkie. Say I was fifteen and
hated my body. Leave out shared hunger,

the heat in the bone flaring so dangerous,
luminous. Something was created.

It was cut out neatly, but at times it comes
with bloody hands. Breaks a window or
two. Announces itself lost. *I was yours.*

The dreams are often of this:
Something is born: a doll with

plastic legs. It will not live, but it might
have. A bowl of hair, the heart of a
rabbit removed still beating.

9.

The car pulled up in front of the Embassy
garden party and gunshots were fired.

The boy whose father would later be assassinated and I
crouched under the wrought iron table,

moss dripping off it, the green drag of summer.
So much we were not to know or speak of.

My mother wept on the upstairs porch over a
letter she found from my father to the other woman;

the other woman who thought he might marry her,
but didn't, because of us. So much that crinkles

around the edges, blackens or warps.
The boy and I held hands while the adults moved

over us. He wore a striped red-and-blue
t-shirt from Sears. Later at his father's funeral

I was afraid to look at him, afraid
of the dream that climbs a staircase

on thief-quiet feet, knifes itself behind the eyes.
Pictures unreeling: the carousel of slides from

Brazil my father showed me the year I came home from
college. Strange that not one ever showed my legs

or did I never let them be shown? Concealed behind
a thickness of ferns, the splayed and patterned

leaves of the rubber plants. What did my mother want
instead? What did my father? I have never been told.

Once, when they had been fighting, he dropped
my sisters and I off at a gilded old movie house on

one of São Paulo's wider boulevards to watch
Sleeping Beauty.

We had seen that cartoon before—the princess singing
to the bluebirds, the three cuddy fairies, but

the cinema was empty, and by the time the show
began, our father was gone. No soundtrack to

speak of—only the cackle of a violin, a scratched
record that stammered, repeated,

only a row of girls in white tulle and tiered wigs,
the Moscow ballet or the one from Prague or Berlin—

the corps dancing *en pointe* in front of a stage
of terrible red curtains. A girl spinning,

falling. A man in a mask sweeping her away
so her feet would not touch. She climbed the stairs

like my worst nightmares, the ones where I would
wake in my own house, and my father would be there,

my mother and he—but I didn't know him,
he didn't know me.

10.

Still it comes back—
like wine through the tendons,
the shape of what
is missing.

I wake in the night wishing
I could unshed so easily
that stubborn kink, curve
of bone.

Good Doctor, the mask of
hero is a heavy burden.
I show you a hole. You
fill it. A crooked limb, which

you will straighten or snap,
as necessary. I know I will
disappoint in the end—under
iridescent flame, a

theatre framed by sterile
curtains, the uncanny light of
your third eye

& how to love
those marks you made,
a line of tracks cutting
the field.

11.

I let go a little at a time. Today the
iteration of, tomorrow the muscle-

memory. When the box is empty, I draw
inside a bird with flapping wings. It will fly

skyscraper-high, I tell you.
You don't ask, and I

seal the box with masking tape. I paint
over it, first blue, then the thinnest

bleach of cloud. Not lenticular—
not cumulous, not mare's tale, but lighter,

fleeting. I name them: "Small moisture
of a pocket," "Inadequate, the linen hand-

kerchief," "O walking rain will
you never strike ground?"

(Hope is a thing with ______.)

II

Istanbul 1983

In the frozen square, the student asks me if I will
sell him the books from my backpack. He hides them
under his winter coat. Steam rises from the whole-
wheat rolls we break open at the breakfast table.
We drink hot apple tea and pronounce the skyline
"charming." In a jail a man counts the visible bones,
and recounts them in the blaze of morning. To turn
a self to light proves painful—each piece must
be dissected in turn; you pass through every feeling
imaginable, so many you might make a dictionary—
dread to disgust, delight to degradation. The prisoner
remembers only a feverish desire for books—
running fingers over pyramids of words as if he might
translate himself from this life to a more vivid existence,
in which he cuts open the pages with a knife in
plain sight of everyone like a man eating meat and
potatoes at the dinner table. Not that world; this one
where blue light and sharpened files, where identikit
and stamps on passports, where the book in his back-
pack is a crime, and I have sold him down the river
for ideas I barely value—the volumes flung carelessly
across my hotel room, while he picks mushrooms on
the edge of dread, pallid ghosts of what won't speak
or be spoken. Or where I remember what it is to
be present in the world, and I turn away, unable to
bear it—so much light and dread, so much in the darkness
growing or simply how hard to ever remain in place.

The Red Shoes

Someone buried red slippers under the floorboards
and the mice nested in them. The floors splintered no matter

how many cans of deck paint we used. And one night
at the Embajada, I broke a tooth, and the very next

night, three teenagers were shot dead as they sat at
a booth by the window eating mofongo. The neighbor

woman used to sing a funny song from the forties
about a road and "clear day," a fast car and a woman

with a pistol. You could see her back had been broken,
and she dragged her left foot behind her down the

stairs to the mailroom. And Junior began smoking
crack after his church on Columbus failed and started

going by his birth name, which was *Jesus,* until he
fell in love with Irma of the hideous rabbit fur-and-

white-leather jacket, who stopped the cars by waving
her watery hands, smoothing her moth-bitten hair

from her moon-pale face, the violet lipstick she
always wore until she wound up drowned in the East

River, and no one would say if it was suicide or
murder. But Junior said there were eels inside her and

began preaching again, doped on the corner. Mr.
Rodriquez fired him, though he didn't want to, and after

Mr. Rodriquez often looked sweaty and pale as he
labored to move stuff to the basement, which he had once

done with Junior to help him. We painted our rooms
cinnamon, Aegean blue, repainted them eggshell, grise-pearl.

We fought, and you tore all my letters and diaries and
sprinkled them out the window where they landed on

the roof of your car, plastered there by a violent
summer storm. It took hours to scrape them off; I wept

and Mr. Rodriquez gave me a small plastic-wrapped
packet of Kleenex, and that autumn you wound up in Saint

Luke's on lockdown. and Junior caught pneumonia,
died that November. He was thirty-eight, though we

had believed him older. They buried him in Calvary
Cemetery in Queens. Once I rode a cab out that way—

we got lost, so many ticking minutes among the
slender white spikes of the graves. The red slippers—

they must have been for dancing, thin-soled as if with
mouseskin, a powder inside that might have been talc,

rosin, or years of plaster dust, a piece of broken ribbon,
black at the edges as if burned off or torn and smeared with

shoe polish. Or the mice had gnawed it. And you
said "The name of the film" and I said I thought it was a

story older by far, a girl who puts on the shoes and cannot
get them off, who skips down a road, then another and

across the world, until her feet fall off, and her hands
and they make her wooden ones.

Maybe this thirteen-year-old with the bruised look around her mouth can really sing because of what she knows, but how does she know so much so soon, in the torn yellow dress, in the basement room. She is speaking of starlings, and the lightest bones of the wren, and to travel through clouds as one of them, vanish into mist and chill, the space where feathers freeze and drop. Or she is singing of orchards and football games and kids in short pants, who throw rocks at cars that pass shacks with tar-paper roofs and smell of coal. Or the man's hands, which have turned to stray dogs, abject and also dangerous. She must know in her bones, she must know from some older place. You almost believe a ghost has entered her, moth she swallowed by mistake, memory river that snaked down inside, along with the rare glass of fresh milk, the scalding coffee, the bourbon she steals in sips from glasses that glitter on bedside tables, in rooms where she is only there to gather up the sheets, dust the corners. You can be so forgotten you shine the night. You can be hit up against a wall. You can go blind and blue, dog-sick. Now, she lifts the needle to the brittle disk. Or she turns the crank for the metal piece with holes in it that sings into the room where everyone is dancing. And when she mouths the word *own*, the moon sinks down like a woman swaying her hip to bounce off he earth and back to her ever-lonely orbit.

If this is a snapshot of time where is she?

in the rain falling slantwise,
toxic orange of streetlights, leather smell of

the backs of yellow cabs,
across the park with my breath against
a fretwork of the
trees,

in the mahogany bar of the
fabled hotel where our drinks cost
ten dollars and came with violet paper umbrellas,

in the alleyways, the high green dumpsters—
in the fruit-rot of summer where

we picked up bottles for quarters,
emptied ashtrays in the latest borrowed apartment,

in July in Coney Island, walking
into the waves,

because we had nothing else to do,
because I knew nothing,
because she repeated my ignorant gestures,

a little flicker—

bird-dark.

Where? How long?

Sublet
(for Susan Hopkins)

The second day, you read the journal
she left, though I begged you not to—

April—quick rains sluicing the roads,
a light of beantrees, trash cans
lined up by the basement door.

Your arm a corded shadow,
tying off, shooting up.

*

In her sink, the sterling forks, Puritan
and spare with their engraved
lilies, shaken over with Comet,
boric acid. A postcard from Oaxaca
a blazing—inked on the back,

a shelf of books on copy-editing,
her cautious sample pages.

*

As if (as if?) I could feel the fates rushing
towards her, a chess set

inexorable and stately,

a room of dominos—a flick of
a wrist and the slow black ripple.

*

I polished her forks,
two at a time. Set them like
Faberge eggs in the royal-blue

velvet box cracking in her one tin
drawer. From her parents' house, which
I stopped to picture—a colonial,
gleaming with cream semi-gloss,
brass end-table lamps.

*

What becomes of the lives we
discard? When I heard she
died, I was not surprised,

but wished I had been.

*

That August—just after we
moved out, she called to ask about

some small missing jewelry. I have
always been thankful I did not

guess: You stripping the lapis enamel
pins from their furred velvet
backings: cloisonné butterfly,
curve of Easter Lily.

Another merely stupid betrayal.

*

And the nights I lay beside you
on her narrow bed, fighting to make
my breathing match yours—

I would call it love, except
I don't think I know enough
to call whatever I felt, to call

whatever I knew.

*

But her. I do think of her,
closer than you. Her wild red curls,

careless female objects—Japanese paper

and the inchoate forms she made
lined up on the bathroom windowsill.

Exit Pursued by Bear
(For Chauvet)

They slept in the Cave of the
Bears. They slept while the bears were
hibernating the winter, fur and

sharp smell. It was like our love,
that room of wet fur and fear,
that room with their strange hearts.

Red-faced men in the bar
speak in taut voices, their hands
turning over. "You wouldn't
want to sleep too soundly,"
"You wouldn't want to forget
all the ways they might wake up."

At the butcher shop, the carcass of
an animal hangs upside down, dripping blood.

At night we draw it,
make necklaces from its teeth
and wear them around our necks.

Rimbaud's Letters

I grew sad those evenings in Butler
Library, the grand collections radiating

out on all sides, those days when
you could still smoke in a library.

He had written the lines I
repeated daily under my breath:

*Le magique etude de bonheur/qu'aucun
elude*. I did not know entirely what

they meant, but I grasped that difficult
study called *happiness*—

white Russians at the Dive Bar, a
stammering before strange boys, waking

in Lynne's rose-nylon slip, or dialing Michele
from the payphone at the corner.

The volume was bound in red morocco.
No one had checked it out for years.

Of certainly limited interest
said the introduction. *We hunt for clues*

and find none. I read slouched on the vinyl
couch by the door where boys and

girls spoke in purring voices, trading numbers
scratched on insides of matchbooks,

a noising from the row of radiators making
you think *engine, engine*. The year Lynne

began to kill herself, and Michele made a
hard marriage. How purely we loved one

another. He wrote about money and guns,
the body. The introduction

said: *Rarely has a writer of such*
greatness written prose of so little interest.

Even then I understood sometimes it
is better to think nothing. In the hallway of

Butler library, seven years and three months
before they would ban smoking utterly,

I filled my lungs and read until the
flat letters spoke to me. What

can I tell you? I still smoke too much, long
to die almost as much as I want to live.

Alchemist of words, he had not forgotten
how to make you breathe in his skin. Only

now he wrote only of the heat, the appalling food
& insects, the desert glare so pellucid

like being pinned by the Sun—prom king so
radiant every kiss means a new death.

Material will out, his letters said.
Hope dies. This is what happens.

Crawl In

I practice rituals of forgiveness, scattering
sage on the threshold or

peeling the wax leavings off the red candle.
None of it quite does

away with the needle that stabs through
at odd moments of the day.

I puzzle as over a photo in a locket, that picture
in my mind. We sit at a table over our poems,

we pass them back and forth, scrawling
messages of encouragement. Ice thickens

the windows, and the trees slowly turn
blue with it, blue and terribly naked.

What did losing you do? I left a home, lost
knowing my place and what objects

around me might mean. Morning: a slight
shiver as rain streaks across the windshield,

and the woman before me in the take-out coffee
drive-through begins pounding

her horn for no reason I can see,
but it's called road rage. I don't utter your name.

Along the river swollen with summer storms,
a willow grows half-in, half-out of the

water, a leafing so intense when I duck under,
though the long twiggy curtains of branches,

I feel quite erased. There is that scene in
the story—we both knew it by heart—

where the witch opens the oven and asks
the girl to crawl in. She doesn't, but we all sense

that moment of hesitation, the green thrust of
a trust that should be able to remain unbroken.

Birthday

Even if I did not dare invite anyone, I still wanted
a party—as in the fountain downtown to change

colors, a saxophone to start noodling out of nowhere,
or simply a friend to sit me down at a table under

striped awnings where chestnut trees bloom.
A girl to recite from a book of dead poems:

holiness, danger, and a smell of lime.
The waiter to bring me coffee the way I like it—

scalding, but not too, the tiny metal pitcher
of chilled milk. I would eat pie—hot with a dab

of ice cream, the crust shattering as it should,
the fruit beneath sour to pucker my lips.

I'd know better than to wish any fairground tricks,
no jolting ascents or swooping falls, only a long dullish read,

a train ride where I might stare out at passing fields—
hayricks, children playing in mud, a town

confettied for some minor regional festival, which
would be my party, the one I throw myself, in

which I whisper to a stranger one true thing—yes,
I know how far I have come—blue edge,

water-wheel churning; yes, the world is a glory,
but always the dust bunnies behind the bureau,

the parts of the self I long to wrap up in old t-shirts
and hide under the bed like a book I fear.

Here, the mornings and middle-of-nights when
I am the cricket sawing its leg to sing.

The Sad Fate of the Sisterhood

I watched her sun lizard-like
at the edge of the university pool.
She wanted in. I watched her flare

like a match in cupped hands—gorgeous
cool flame. We exchanged tricks,
recipes, the gossip of sisterly closeness.

The trick is how the blade appears, how
history is carved in the flick of
a wrist. She grows ever

my stranger. I believe she feels
the same sickness—the flummery,
the twaddle, so much disposable.

At times, her desolation is almost real
to me, the sly blue of a vein
we recalled ourselves opening—

red ruby, bead-by-bead, the violent
means by which we would turn the insides out,
hoping someone would proclaim them pretty.

Breaking the Wishbone

Who is calling *cut*? Who breaks
the thin bone and hands you a piece?

I like the almost stagy scene—the hero
cupping her cheek, or the one where she walks
the coast road, skirts whipping around her legs.

Lamp-bright, fade to black where I am
sitting on the couch, and wrong
and wrong again. But here's a little
slit into a purer space. Her husband
is a spy who poisons her—

don't trust your heart to a man
with broad shoulders.
She has a happy ending; in life
it would not happen in time, or would not stay.

The trees whip so startlingly by
her car window one almost imagines
they might pull themselves
out by the roots. I love that
she's drunk and mooning at them.

I love that he has to rescue her.
I love that she almost dies.

And what have I chosen to care for?
You, across from me, sawing the carcass of the bird
we roasted, boiled, you,

someone I never quite see,
plucking clean for us this tiny hair-pin bone.

Confessional Ballad

1.

My gift, to turn you to stone—
clear yet murky-dark, clear and

fathomless at the same time. I could
parse your hands on a table for

almost eternity, turn myself into
blue bruise, ragged flower,

chicory stalk by the railroad tracks.

I could will myself into glass pane,

clear yet able to shatter and wound.
I could rise covered with tiny

glass slits, holes I name after
each of your moods, each instance

of you unreeling as a film—
illusory light, quickening what is

over-and-out, dead-and-gone like
Hank in the back of his cold truck,

the engine gilly-flower blue,
lead-blue, dreadful-blue, and his high

voice that sings to me here.

2.

Blue eyes, blinking in the sky,
and the curlew cawing in slow waves,

the bitten edges of the gutter-
choke leaves, the high-summer

mustard, winking at its sister.

3.

Blue eyes in puddles, within delicate

cases of stone-flies. I built something—it
was like a nest—baby hair,

strings of gilt. Anything can be crushed,
and the sign is not in the thing,

but in the sweet-poison pill,
capsule holding what-never-was or

what-almost-became. The apples in
my bottom drawer wrinkle,

give off a memory smell. I write you
postcards because they cause less pain,

produce no obligation to reply.

The Artifacts
(for Andrew)

Last night on the phone you
said to me "The boy burned the house
down because that was where

the crazy people lived." In my head,
a picture of us years ago, striding the
length of Claremont Avenue. The

powdered coffee we made in the mornings,
proud of our thrift. Our riches—
the simple ones of believing the body

would always be this good. You stood
outside in your socks and watched
the flames, smell of plastic streaming

the air. At odd times, a memory
retrieves itself; the cells shiver a little
and wake. Remember the Klezmer player

on the 125th Street Station platform, the
beaver hat he wore to catch our dimes? Why
did we never hear the swoon in the

melodies he played—din of a people
torn by pogroms. You stood outside for
an hour or more before they took you

to the shelter. And the snow, it fell
in feathers and notes, a hush on the purple
majestic skies, skies of middle-of-

night, *black milk we drink like*
morning, the grief of the good body,
which remembers everything.

Finding Feathers

We know there was a
murder; it happened at a moment
indistinguishable

from the others—a bird
took flight, midnight in its
feathers, the sun rolled over,

light struck a metal cage
with unusual force. Think of it
like dew falling with

no one to observe it. Now
the leaves all aglitter, the
mercury descending—

ferocious, the plummet,
down and straight as the
lead at the base of any

chain. We don't know how
to rewind from winter. What
we know is waiting—

to jar the fruits, each
suspended in an amber
syrup: Wax chamber, sugar

nest. Even as these are
distanced, they twinkle in the
cellar. We are always giving

birth to stars, flaming and
burning out. The feather
in the hand, which

as in a fairy tale speaks of
the winged soul—and it rises,
I tell you, it rises with

such force. No one
can stop the spring any
more than halt winter,

and in our skies these
traces, journeys. The birds
have vanished now.

III

For Avalon

We know better than
present-tense

the velvet of recede—

hands wave useless
dictions

the mouth as you find it:
a blood-rag

the body ever the scar
of itself and if

I had just once, I had—

what rift? The body
always separating each

from each, self from self
& so I write you still:

I could not breathe then.
I could not keep breathing.

The Fable of Demeter and Persephone

In the hospital of sad princesses,
they walk with their feet
pointed outward, their washboard
stomachs. They weave friendship
bracelets of violet and crimson lake,
bend their heads like swans
to half-empty cups of water in
which they never see themselves.

Not once. Six glowing jeweled
seed are clasped in every hand.
Nights, they picture the earth heaved
open, themselves on the pale throne,
judging souls. Their mothers must wander
the world, carting wheelbarrows of
pumpkins that have lost their stems,
whatever might connect them to the
wormy soil. Their daughters know
what lives down there—what fire
can exist in the chill core of any

stone. They care only for what lasts
while their mothers weep over fields
where winter strips every
leaf. In the hospital of sad princesses,
they perform a pageant every day
for the miracle of ice, what strength
in a land where nothing will grow—
planetary florescence of sapphire, emerald,
the trees of the underworld whose
beautiful fruit would break anyone's
teeth. It is not so different from any
game of chicken—the car speeds towards
you, and you hold a pose, sing the
weeping willow, the singing head that floats,

the River Lethe, which murmurs on,
swallowing everything that has
ever been. O dark mouth of the world,
here is where all mothers and daughters
split. How can the girls not despise
that the mothers will make a meal of
anything—even them?

About Snakes

I would lie if I said it was easy—
if I neglected to tell how I thrashed about
after, fingering my bite, which
stained me so inside—my soil
parched, the tomato plants felled by

curly top. Pecans shedding
their nuts too soon,
a hot wind, their blank brains, until I

haunted the alleys,
slashes of shade in garages,

dreamed nightly of a water that would
silver over me, make me more like them,
or better able to live in their company.

When the monsoons came,
I flung my arms out
to grasp every last drop, a thing
I had never done before.
Maybe it was balm after all to learn
that I was not
the center of anything.

How many rains had passed
in a blur? How many minds had I believed
like my own? There's
a door in a wall at the end of a dirt road,
to a garden where every-

thing is only itself—
the candle of ocotillo,
and—who knows why?—

that diamond-
backed God coiled around the trunk.

Perdurable
Very durable; lasting; continuing long.

From the Fr. *Perdre*: "To lose?"
If so I must love it for containing "to
lose" so neatly, so completely—what
can be held like the lily-pad
floating the surface—that lake of loss,
so limpid as it blindly reflects
frost-blue sky, shift of cloud.

"Continuing long," which
means *not forever*, which means
your shoulder against my teeth—
ivory-gleam, crenellated country.
A kind of cheat that the word might speak so
eloquently the loss it appears to forestall.

You are *perdurable* to me—cleft of
lip, fat tongue, desire which falls
and glosses like rain this dry land
in which I learn daily what *long* means.
the dust of how and in what
measure.

Idle Chat

Today you put on your dark glasses as if the words hurt you. What would seeing your eyes do for me? You e-mail me sometimes that we should meet for coffee or idle chat, but nothing feels idle here, not even our hands, which tear at napkins or matchbooks for no apparent reason. *Be restful, be restive.* I watch the leaves across the patio; how lovely that they are swept from side to side with no apparent rhyme or reason. Sadness is floating on this matter as it occurs in our everyday lives. What was it they said about idle hands? What did they mean the devil's workshop? When the world fills me, I tell you, I like to go drive. I tell you about the shrikes on the chicken wire fences, the hawks that ride any windshear. We agree there is nothing in the world like the smell of creosote after rain, the blooms of the soap-plant, so tall and thrusting upward, or the ocotillo, like a man burning up by himself in the middle of a field.

We're All Optimists Here

The light that shines over the damp
rooftop, frozen yards is weightless.
Weightless, the twigs above,

splayed like the bones in a hand,
and the breath of the three men
waiting for the morning bus, their

cupped hands, wet wool jackets.
Or this book I take from my shelf—
Guy de Maupassant, who wrote scenes

of such crystalline clarity—
garrisons and ballrooms, the train car
where the peasant woman nurses

the starving soldier. Maupassant
died crawling across a floor,
unable to remember even

his name. And the story that ends
in Maupassant's death was written
by Isaac Babel, never seen

after 1941, shot in one of 476 camps
of the Gulag, his bones lost
in Norvisk, Volkota, or far

Kolyna. Across the street, a boy
cuts caddy-corner across a lawn.
The grass he tramples is demure as

a bridal veil—no longer alive, not
dead either. And the knowledge that
touches Babel with light fingers,

what he reads in Maupassant shitting
himself on the floor, is simply
no protection. Somewhere someone

is dying who never wrote even
a letter—watery song
inside the breath of sky.

Babel's heavy script: *no*
iron touches the heart like a period
in exactly the right place.

Bare Ruined Orchards

In the road
of the trees there are
no corners. You might
flit for a long
time, forget the

direction you
intended—drown in a
sea of verdigris,
a blizzard of
crackling.

Leaves unfurl,
break off,
drift to earth. If
there is a clock,
it is not

in synch with
any other—it is
the timer of now-
an-apple-is-almost,
now-a-caterpillar-is
-about-to. And

the seasons each
take a long time to finish,
though they have
a progression—

stately as dancers
approaching in a
contradance,
the weaving hands and
nimble feet.

Keeping up is breathless.
Autumn: the stripped
branches,
intoxicating scent of
barrel after barrel—

Pippens, Ashmead's
Kernel, Winesap,
and

Jonathan,
Northern Spy. I used
to name each thing
with care, then in the road
of the trees forget them
one at a time.

The Burning Boy

I read the news about a boy and
his horse set on fire on the border by
Palomas. I felt like him, my hair crackling,
or him after, the dryness of what
has been irrevocably burned to ash.

What they don't tell you about middle
age—it will feel like youth burning,
the same river twice, desire turning
and flashing silver in the setting sun, or
the tiny fish, which keep slipping through

your fingers, their loss made sharper by
the weight of what you know. No one
innocent, no one true. Not even you, though
you try so mightily. Today a friend wrote
me an injured e-mail, which I deserved. I

had dispatched him so efficiently, the way
I cut bread for sandwiches, the serrated edge
of a knife, wrapping them tight in plastic
not enough like skin, the crumb-strewn
table I wipe sterile-clean, keep wiping.

The boy kept riding for five minutes—flare
of such agony, my hand shakes imagining it.
I carry him in my head; I can't help it. And I know
there is terrible courage in even the smallest
weight of time. I think tonight of my hurt

friend, my sorry self. I think of all the things I
have not done right. My snug house ticking
beside the denuded canal. The horse rearing up,
the boy screaming. And you who I have

loved in such a way it has only made me
less kind. A cloud of mosquitoes swirls over
the acequia. If I walked out there, they would
bloody my legs, but here, though the window
screen, they are breathtaking—bright thistle,
gold cloud that flickers with dark lights.

Tristia

You signed the card "Zeus
always." *Thanks for everything.*

When I met you and your hand
did that shaky thing, I baked

biscuits. I imagined
the steam would mend you.

Instead it proved a cloud, wrapping
me in a fog so thick I could no

longer put on my own shadow:
Zeus—endless in the sky, who

makes the trees at the end of the yard
waver like water. I remembered

the women who heard Pan fingering
his flute from the heart of the wood,

left their pots untended, houses
to burn, tearing off their clothes

to dance themselves dumb.
Why couldn't I see how powerful you were?

Riding bare-backed over the fields,
so turned in you had nothing

to give. The God never lets us know
how he is woven into every thing,

but we never let him know how
cleverly we try to unmake him.

I shook the trees until the birds inside
them flew off—the leaves fell

away. I swept them in piles and
left them bagged on the curb.

I gave the postcard to my daughter
to cut up.

Frozen

We did not see my sister slip away
into the mythic world of air, ice, and hunger
until it was almost too late. I did not
see my daughter do the same until her
arms were twigs in the photographs which see
more than we do. Time stilled in the picture
on the lawn where she—my daughter as
did my sister once—leans back into the
shadow of a spring tree—
a magnolia not yet thick and floral, an aspen
quaking yellow on a slight hill, a rubber
plant, each leaf streaked like veins, and the
story of the photograph never quite the same
as the story of the heart or how it stutters
and tries to uncover each time a new
language. She won't listen when we tell her
to eat; in the photographs we take, her
face translucent and also clouded, lower lip
pushed out, palms facing us as if to say
"Go, go away." Some of the old photographs
fool me every time. Everyone is smiling and
you don't see the storms of father or
mother who wished we did not cling so tight
as I wish it now, trying to pull back my child
so hard my body turns hollow, a shell, a
case of stitched skins. If the photograph could
only give us the selves we know—their torturous
journeys and mythic panopticons. Perhaps then
I would understand why my daughter refuses
to eat. Her "no" so obdurate we
are forced to prison her within this frame:
A photograph, a plate, three times a
day, a meal, each one laid out so carefully:
the meat, the potatoes, the greens. But she doesn't

live here. The photograph can't tell us what
she sees—and that other world, hers, so full of
rules that must be followed, prohibitions, rituals,
glittering and immaculate as the ice crystals,
which even now form in the mornings on the
windows of our house—small starbursts like memories
of breath. She must love so much the notion
of unchanging. She touches them with cold fingers.
In the photograph, we can see her carving—the
terrible art of turning herself to air.

Morning

Cheat grass is spread
over concrete like corn for a chicken,
and the sky lightens,
a series of bandages being
unwrapped from a
wound. At first I wake as into

water, as into nothing; then I
I remember you again, and love plucks
me back like cheat
grass in my hands, or a glass I have
broken, and the tiny
splinters that glitter and mix,

sand-dust and blood. If you
came back I imagine I would smell you
like pine tree, and
I would not know what to say,
my hands fluttering around
me like birds whose home-tree

is burning. And I wish
it were not like this, but who
would I be without this burden?
How would I know myself
without this longing, which
is unanswerable as sky or the noising

of so much and more life
in the bushes, each aspen,
the bladed grass.
I am holding myself tight
and walking into it as I used to
walk into the still pond

at my friend's house in the Catskills,
and when the mud stirred up
from the bottom, the water

clouded with green. I could say love is
only a confusion, and
also what we are made for, the pieces

of us bleeding up.

Parable of the Birds

Morning damp—the dawn and someone has to sing.

I say jokingly we are in end-game, planet whirling, warming like a ball passed between too many eager hands.

Remember the hawk circling the dead possum on the fresh tarmac road?

Flush of willow by a creek—blood-mesquite, the wild osier?

The trees thicken like fingers.

They want so much and hoard what they get, the jeweled sap-flow, and the grasses spilling, even now, over the bitten concrete edges of where we live.

I would make us a nest of straws.

I would untie our shoes and leave them as a warning.

Here sometimes we spot circles of fire where migrants burn what they came with.

The gasoline ripple, the siren song of becoming someone new.

I never believed I would be reborn as a bird, but at night I dream of hard flight.

I have to labor and strain just to rise a few feet—and amazing how fast the world thins.

Rapture

1.

The word was an ache—
a green that breaks

through a furrow,
the fields, the bone-

meal, how it burned.

2.

I was holding

in my head a small drunk sun, which was not you,
but like you, because around it

I felt my self alight, *raptus,* the bird that floats
thermals,

before descending so abruptly
with only one intent.

3.

Later, ashes,
condors, the fields a mess, and

maybe I did not want to know what would grow
from this: my—our—*rapio,* a

"carting off by force."

4.

Me: moving-alive, never a

respite, respiring,
a paroxysm for any raptor—

that silvered earth, a shudder in which the
weak is blood-impulsive,
and it gets snatched, impaled.

5.

Your jest
of tendered hand, mine of the throat,

the way to imagine belonging
is to set oneself
against another thing,

Migrant

Nothing lives here any more but
she carries love like water, a cup,

a small shot-glass. She climbs
the stairs, she takes the hot tray

with flowers, she leaves the patient
asleep, she sheds her shoes

and crosses the field sideways. She
stares at the cows chewing blind,

imagines their life in desert stockades,
studies every sky for signs of

rain—the kind that falls, drying before
it strikes earth. She carries a

small pen, the ability to reframe.
She carries a taut coil of wire,

the compulsion to build her fence
wherever she goes. The secret of

borders is that they beg a crossing;
the secret of water is it must spill,

seep, and darken; the secret of
love is that it must divide, and she stares

at the garden, where she learns,
even here, under the brutal sun, that

whatever will not shrivel must grow.

Acknowledgements

The author expresses her gratitude to the editors of the following publications in which some of these poems first appeared:

Antiphon, Birmingham Review, Blackbox Manifold, Bluestem, Burnt District, Conclave, Conte, Cutbank, Cutthroat, The Destroyer, Diode, The Guardian Poetry Workshop, I-70 Review, Ink Pot, Lunch Ticket, Mas Tequila Review, MiPoesis, New Sound Review, Poetry Magazine, Qarrtsiluni, San Antonio Express-News, So to Speak, Split this Rock Blogspot, Spry, Sweet, Sugared Water, Talking Poetry, Tyger Burning, Typo, Watershed Review, WomenWriters.Net, Wordgathering

"Migrant" and "Hope is a Thing With _____" (part of "Iron, Ardent") received Pushcart Prize nominations.

Thanks to Duncan, Annabelle, Walker, Eliza, sisters Samantha and Sarah, parents Clay and Moira.

For their friendship and help with this book the author would also like to thank:

Louis Asekoff, Wendy Barker, Jennifer Bartlett, Jenny Browne, John Lee Clark, Debra Magpie Earling, Laurie Ann Guerrero, Laura Healy, Tony Hoagland, Craig Holden, Susannah Hollister, Melissa Kwasny, Jen Knox, Dana Kroos, Jim LaVilla-Havelin, Allison Layfield, David Levinson, Denise Leto, Philip Levine, Michele Marcoux, Candice Marrow, Marnie Nixon, Michael Northen, Sharon Olinka, Anisa Onofre, Laurie Posner, Octavio Quintanilla, Barbara Ras, Evelyn Reyes, Bernadette Smyth, Carrie Tafoya, Lynne Thermann, Viktoria Valenzuela, Alexandra van de Kamp, Laura Van Prooyen, Ben Tremillo, Natalia Trevino, Joe Vastano, Connie Voisine, Joni Wallace, Amanda Ward, and George Ypsilantis.

About the Author

Sheila Black is the author of *House of Bone* and *Love/Iraq,* (both from CW Press), and *Wen Kroy* winner of the 2011 Orphic Prize in Poetry from Dream Horse Press. She is a co-editor with Jennifer Bartlett and Michael Northen of *Beauty is a Verb: The New Poetry of Disability*, (Cinco Puntos Press). She received a 2012 Witter Bynner Fellowship from the Library of Congress, for which she was selected by Philip Levine. She lives in San Antonio, Texas where she directs Gemini Ink, a literary arts center.

Made in the USA
Charleston, SC
27 January 2017